POSTCARDS OF HOPE

The Bible Reading Fellowship
15 The Chambers, Vineyard
Abingdon OX14 3FE
brf.org.uk

The Bible Reading Fellowship (BRF) is a Registered Charity (233280)

ISBN 978 0 85746 648 8
First published 2018
10 9 8 7 6 5 4 3 2 1 0
All rights reserved

Text and illustrations © Ellie Hart 2018
Back cover texture © Thinkstock
This edition © The Bible Reading Fellowship 2018

The author asserts the moral right to be identified as the author of this work

Acknowledgements
Unless otherwise acknowledged, scripture quotations are taken from The Holy Bible, New International Version (Anglicised edition) copyright © 1979, 1984, 2011 by Biblica. Used by permission of Hodder & Stoughton Publishers, a Hachette UK company. All rights reserved. 'NIV' is a registered trademark of Biblica. UK trademark number 1448790. • Scripture quotations are taken from The Message, copyright © 1993, 1994, 1995, 1996, 2000, 2001, 2002 by Eugene H. Peterson. Used by permission of NavPress. All rights reserved. Represented by Tyndale House Publishers, Inc. • Scripture quotations from The New Revised Standard Version of the Bible, Anglicised edition, copyright © 1989, 1995 by the Division of Christian Education of the National Council of the Churches of Christ in the United States of America. Used by permission. All rights reserved.

Every effort has been made to trace and contact copyright owners for material used in this resource. We apologise for any inadvertent omissions or errors, and would ask those concerned to contact us so that full acknowledgement can be made in the future.

A catalogue record for this book is available from the British Library

Printed and bound by The Graphic Design House, Portsmouth PO6 1TR

POSTCARDS
OF HOPE

Words and pictures to breathe life into your heart

Ellie Hart

Hope /həʊp/: **n.** An optimistic attitude of mind, based on the expectation of positive outcomes.

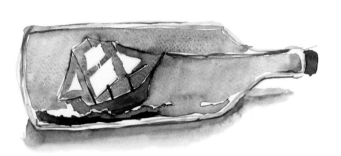

Introduction

We have this hope as an anchor for the soul, firm and secure.
It enters the inner sanctuary, behind the curtain, where our
forerunner, Jesus, has entered on our behalf.
HEBREWS 6:19–20

I hear a lot about hope: how we need it to survive, how people cling to it, how painful it is to have lost it. The Bible describes it as an anchor for the soul; something to keep you steady and secure, perhaps even on a stormy sea.

Hope is extraordinarily powerful, but if it is shown to be false, the disappointment can be utterly crushing. We all need to anchor our souls to something beyond ourselves, but when you're being tossed about by the waves, having your hope-rope tied to anything that is in this world is just like being anchored to another set of waves; there's no guarantee of stability coming.

And yet true hope, the hope that the Bible holds out to us, is in a different league altogether. As Hebrews tells us, it is anchored not in this world, but on the other side of the curtain, in the place where Jesus has gone ahead of us, in the presence of God.

I may be like a tiny boat on a vast ocean but deep, deep down and beyond, I am fixed irrevocably to something other than more waves: something solid and unmoveable; something which contains the ocean itself.

A while ago, God spoke to me about starting to write postcards of hope – pictures with a message on the back that would be little bursts of real, solid hope for a world that needs it more than ever.

I wonder if you've ever watched someone make a ship in a bottle? The crafter makes the little boat in pieces, with its masts and sails on tiny hinges so that it can fold up, becoming slender enough to slip in through the neck of the bottle. Once it's inside and fixed into place, he pulls on the very fine threads and gently raises the mast, unfurling the sails to fill the space.

My prayer is that as you read these postcards, God would use the stories and pictures to slide truth gently into your heart. Once it's in there, may he slowly and gently unfurl its sails so that it spreads out and becomes a part of who you are: hope anchoring you to the Rock.

Ellie Hart

A burst of yellow flowers

It was as if a painter had knocked over a huge tin of bright yellow paint and splashes of it had ended up all over the city.

For most of the year, there is no water at all visible in the little creek that runs through the outskirts of town. The riverbed and the fields around it are dry and bare, with only the dull green of eucalyptus and olive trees to break up the grey-white of rocks and dust.

But this particular winter, rain had fallen. Days and days of it and melting snow from the mountains had swelled the dried-up river from a tiny trickle to a babbling brook.

And then, just as the rain slowed and the sun reappeared, came a burst of yellow wildflowers, gathered together, dancing in the spring breeze and refusing to be ignored.

It's wonderful to realise that spring is coming, that a winter season is past, but it's easy to forget that the flowers that make my heart sing are there as a direct result of the cloud and rain of the winter months.

Life isn't always springtime, but for those of you who don't see the flowers yet, for those of you who are still living in a season of cloudy skies, rain or storms, hear this: the flowers are coming.

The seeds are deep in the ground but soaking up the rain, and the day is coming when the warmth of the presence of God will call them to burst out in your life. Before you know it, they'll be springing up in unexpected places, nodding gently in the gaps in the garage forecourt, spilling out across patches of wasteland and partying wildly in newly green fields.

I don't always have the ability to see it coming – but I do know that eventually the day comes when Jesus calls out to me and to you:

> *Arise, my darling,*
> *my beautiful one, come with me.*
> *See! The winter is past;*
> *the rains are over and gone.*
> *Flowers appear on the earth.*
> SONG OF SONGS 2:10–12

FOR YOUR *JOURNAL*

What kind of season are you in right now?

True hope comes from meditating on the expectation of the positive outcomes that we have to look forward to in Jesus. Look through Ephesians 1 and see what 'yellow flowers' you can find in there.

How does the season you're in look or feel different in the light of the promises of the future?

Brownies

Did you know that when the recipe for chocolate brownies first hit the UK, it caused great confusion and disappointment? It's true. Bakers all over the country found the brownies wouldn't cook 'properly' and didn't turn out as expected. People thought there must have been a terrible error in the recipe – it took Brits a while to learn that squidgy can be a good thing in a cake.

Sometimes life is like this: ministry, family, jobs, health, security, etc. just don't turn out as we expected and planned. Sometimes this is because of our mistakes, or someone else's; often it's because we live in a broken world; and perhaps sometimes it's because, like the brownies, they were never supposed to be the way we'd imagined.

The truth is that more or less everyone is living a different life to the one they'd expected. Even those whose social media might suggest otherwise are facing trials behind the scenes, because life is, on the whole, neither fair nor easy. The rain falls.

But God is good, and with us, and there is an alternative to disappointment, confusion and resentment. There has to be, because those things will eat you up from the inside.

It's this:

You eat the brownies.

They might not be quite what you expected, but they do taste good.

I know many of you are facing situations so hard you can barely stand up. Sometimes life isn't good. Sometimes it's so far away from what you'd hoped it would be that it makes you grieve in the depths of your soul for what might have been.

Mostly, we don't get a lot of choice over which life we live, but we do have a choice in how we face our unexpected lives and how we adjust our attitude towards them.

Perhaps today we can acknowledge that our 'brownies' are not what we expected, not what we asked for or hoped for; but perhaps we can pull together the courage, take a breath, reach for God's hand and eat them.

I hope you will find that, in some unexpected way, they are good.

I had a dream,
I had a plan,
I had a hope,
and courage,
and they haven't turned out as I expected.
Breathe on my dreams,
because you have a plan
and that gives me enough hope
and courage
to live for your glory even in the unexpected.

FOR YOUR *JOURNAL* ————————

Has your life turned out as you expected?

What particular situations or disappointments do you need courage to face just now?

In what ways is your life still good?

Ask God to help you see how you can still live a life that is good and brings glory to him even in the middle of its unexpectedness.

The red dot

'I wonder what that means?'

As we walked around the exhibition, I noticed that a few of the paintings were marked with a bright red sticky dot. Small, but bright. Obvious.

I found out later that each dot marked a painting that had been picked by a buyer and paid for. Ownership had been transferred but, so that the paintings could remain hanging as part of the exhibition, collection had been deferred to the last day of the show.

> *… the Holy Spirit of God, with whom you were sealed for the day of redemption.*
> EPHESIANS 4:30

The Holy Spirit in our lives is like the red dot at an art exhibition. When we believe and trust in Jesus, we are instantly marked out for redemption. His presence shows that we are 'already paid for'. Ownership has been transferred; we are only awaiting collection on the final day.

It's a picture brimming over with grace. There is absolutely nothing I can do (or not do) to affect my status. I have been bought; the required price has been paid: *I belong to God*.

And I wonder to myself: if I really believed this, if I *knew* it in the deep places of my heart, how would I live?

Perhaps I could rest in that truth: it is done. *I am sealed for the day of redemption*.

Perhaps I could stop worrying what God thinks about my multiple mess-ups. *He knows… He bought me*.

Perhaps I could stop striving, working hard to earn his favour. *I belong to him… I can't change the ending*.

And perhaps I could use that confidence and freedom to serve him from my heart instead of my head. *I belong to God… He will be coming back to collect me*.

Father, thank you that you chose me,
that you valued me,
paid the price and bought me,
that I belong to you.
Spirit of wisdom and revelation,
unfold this truth in the deep places of my heart.

FOR YOUR *JOURNAL* ———————————

What do you think resting in this truth that God has redeemed us would look like for you?

How would it change the way you feel and how would that change the way you act?

Jugs

I've got a bit of a weakness for jugs – delicate china ones, sturdy earthenware ones and the bright colourful kind with unglazed bases. I'm drawn to the gorgeous duet of beauty and usefulness.

The jugs in my house each have a different character, are made of different materials and are different sizes. My favourites are the ones that are worn by time or have blemishes in the glaze that make them unique. I use them for different jobs, but they all have the same basic purpose: to be filled up with something and then to pour that something out.

Each of us is like one of these: a handmade, blemished-but-beautiful jug, and God has written a beautiful and practical calling in each of our hearts: to be a continual outpouring of God's love, grace and power to whoever he has put us near.

But we can't only be pourers; it simply doesn't work. Like jugs, we are made both for pouring out and for filling up. And it's pretty obvious which needs to happen first. If I put the almost-empty water jug on the dinner table and think to myself, 'I'll fill it up again after I've poured out all the drinks,' it simply won't work. I have to take the time first to fill it up, almost to overflowing, and then do my pouring out of that fullness. Our lives need to have a beautiful balance of being filled and of pouring out. Don't forget that the jug that is always looking to be filled but never pours out is also missing the point.

Maybe you need to come to God today and ask him again to pour out his abundance into your emptiness, to fill you to overflowing, so that you can pour out and be a blessing to others.

Father, I come to you broken,
wondering if you can help me to mend.
Jesus, I come to you full
of own concerns and dreams and plans,
needing you to help me make room for yours.
Spirit, I come to you empty,
acknowledging that I've run dry and have nothing left to give,
knowing that I was designed to be full of you.

God of all mercy, mend my brokenness, empty my fullness, fill my emptiness
and let me be poured out for your glory, over and over again.

FOR YOUR *JOURNAL* ————————

Who has God put you near? Who is he calling you to be an outpouring of his grace, power and love to?

Are you someone who comes back to Jesus regularly to be refilled, or do you run down to empty before you call out to him?

What do you need to do to establish a healthy rhythm of being filled and pouring out in your life?

The art of balancing oranges

Sometimes my life feels a lot like this – balancing oranges. There are so many things yelling for my urgent attention, so many people that need me to do something or be somewhere or find their shoes.

There are days when I think that if someone tries to balance one more orange on top of the pile (just one more), I might yell, throw the whole lot up into the air and storm off.

I don't, of course. I just keep on balancing and dropping. And avoiding people who might have oranges in their pockets they might want me to carry.

I've learned over the years that it helps to pray about things. So I was moaning to God the other day about all the problems and worries and things to do (he called some of them blessings and opportunities, but I wasn't in a totally positive frame of mind), and telling him how I really needed *fewer* oranges, thank you very much, or I couldn't be held responsible for the mess I was going to make on the pavement – when he suddenly stilled my heart and whispered a word of great wisdom and encouragement:

'Get a bigger plate.'

'There are bigger plates?' I asked incredulously. 'I hadn't thought of *that*.'

How to get a bigger plate:

1 Take care of yourself mentally and physically, as much as you are able. It makes a difference.
2 Pray! Walk as closely to Jesus as you can, not as far away as you can get away with. Take time in God's presence every day, even if it's just a little bit.
3 Choose wisely. Ask for wisdom so that you can make good choices and walk in them. Don't try to be a superhero; it might finish you off.
4 Finally, grow your faith. Faith looks fragile but goes granite-hard just as you step out on to it. It gets stronger, wider and more weight-bearing the more you use it, so do.

I pray that if you are balancing oranges, you'll find ways to grow a bigger plate; that your current burden would become a breeze to balance; and that you would be able to learn to let Jesus take responsibility for the weight. I pray also for those days when oranges fall, that you would be enveloped in a grace that enables you to trust our Good Father – the ultimate expert fruit-catcher.

FOR YOUR *JOURNAL* —————————

What are the oranges in your life at the moment?

What things are getting dropped?

What things would you like to be able to say 'yes' to?

Out of faith, wisdom, prayer and health, which do you think will grow your plate? Which would be the biggest challenge to invest in?

Aaron's staff

As I write, the almond buds are about to burst out on the trees in my city. Thousands of white flowers dusted in pink will dance in the breeze, heralding the end of the cold, damp winter and the beginning of spring. None of them will look quite like this picture of Aaron's staff, though.

I wonder what the leaders of the tribes of Israel were expecting as they waited for Moses to bring them back their staffs. I imagine they were somewhat surprised.

Overnight, the dead wood of Aaron's staff, resting in the presence of God, had not only sprouted but budded, blossomed and produced almonds (read the story in Numbers 17). Not only had life miraculously appeared, but the process of budding to blossoming to producing fruit to being ready to harvest (which usually takes from late February until mid-August) had all happened in just one day.

I often put limits on what I expect God to be able to do or the time frame he will work in. This person that I love seems to be beyond his reach; this harvest might happen, but it will probably take a very long time.

The message of this postcard is simply that God *is* life.

And because unstoppable, limitless, powerful life is part of who he is, there are no limits on where he can choose to let that life break out; no limits to what he can restore; no limits to how fast he can do it.

Do you know people or situations that seem utterly beyond hope?
They aren't. God is life.

Do you wonder whether God can do
the impossible things he's been whispering to you about?
He can. He is life.

Do you look at your own heart
and fear that parts of it are never going to beat again?
They will. He is life.

He can take even dead wood and make it fragrant, beautiful and fruitful,
sometimes all at the same time.
It just needs to rest in his presence. He is LIFE.

FOR YOUR *JOURNAL* ——————

What are the situations or people that come to mind when you read this?

Are there parts of your own heart or life that seem lifeless and need a touch from God?

Can you remember any times in the past when God brought life, fragrance, beauty or fruitfulness into places or situations you had lost hope for?

Bring all of these people or situations into his presence now through prayer.

Leaning

As my eight-year-old's favourite movie tells me: 'The world isn't all cupcakes and rainbows' (from *Trolls*, 2016).

But I still sometimes find myself wondering why God leads me into difficult places. I'm not massively resilient, or patient, or strong; I hate change, I care too much about what people think and I have to fight a tendency to want to run away from confrontation and hide under my bed. I am weak.

Many of you will be fighting a battle that is leaving you feeling weak and wounded. Perhaps you too question whether you're the right person for the job. Maybe you're asking God why he didn't pick someone stronger, someone more resilient, someone who could forge this raging river victoriously and energetically and well.

When I read the Bible, I realise that I'm not the only one asking this question. I find Gideon, shivering with fear as he hides in the winepress, so confused by the angel addressing him as a mighty warrior you can almost see him looking over his shoulder to see who the angel could be talking to. 'Save Israel… How can I?'

Why did God pick the weakest man in the weakest family in the weakest tribe in all of Israel to lead his army?

Well, here's a clue, right at the end of the Song of Songs. It's also where the title of this postcard came from:

Who is this coming up from the wilderness
leaning on her beloved?
SONG OF SONGS 8:5

God chooses the weak because they are the ones who learn how to depend on him.

The strong fight in their own strength, but those who limp, lean.

In your fight, or your walk through the wilderness, lean into God. That's how your weakness can become his strength, and his strength can be made complete.

And this will be the end of your story too: you will come up out of this wilderness, and you'll still be leaning.

Come to me,
all you who are weary and burdened,
and I will give you rest.
MATTHEW 11:28

FOR YOUR *JOURNAL* ———————

Are you fighting a battle or travelling through a wilderness at the moment?

What can you do to help you to lean into Jesus more?

How do you think you can learn to lean more, even when you're not limping?

I have loved

I've never liked goodbyes. When my daughter was little, she would refuse even to say the word, as if by not acknowledging someone's departure she could somehow prevent it from happening. There are days when I wish I could work that kind of magic myself.

But goodbyes, and the grief that accompanies them, are a part of life that we can't avoid. Friends move away, children leave home, people precious to us die.

It hurts to say goodbye. And sometimes a little voice whispers that it would be safer to love less; not to invest pieces of my heart in friendships with people who will inevitably leave; that this sadness and sense of loss are signs of a failure to guard my heart, or of weakness.

In some cultures, people know how to grieve well, but I feel we have lost touch with that a bit in the west. We treat grief of all kinds like an illness, something mysterious that we need to get over as quickly as we can and avoid wherever possible.

And yet grief isn't a malfunction. It's not a sign that something is broken and needs fixing. It's actually the reverse. It's a sign that you have done what you were supposed to do, a medal of honour to say that you have loved.

It reminds me of those well-known verses from Ecclesiastes:

There is a time for everything,
and a season for every activity under the heavens:
a time to be born and a time to die,
a time to plant and a time to uproot,
a time to kill and a time to heal,
a time to tear down and a time to build,
a time to weep and a time to laugh,
a time to mourn and a time to dance.

ECCLESIASTES 3:1–4

This is how life is. Goodbyes and grief happen. There are seasons when weeping and mourning and perhaps even anger are the appropriate emotions to feel and to express. But I love how these verses from Ecclesiastes form a piece of poetry that sparkles with hope. There will also be seasons of healing and building, laughing and dancing to come, at the right time.

Remember this the next time you have to say a goodbye, or when you're mourning for whatever reason. You may not want to do it loudly, but do it without shame.

Wear it as a medal of honour – 'I have loved.'

*FOR YOUR **JOURNAL*** ——————————

How do you feel about saying goodbye to people, places or stages of life?

How can you treat your own grief and other people's with more grace?

Orienteering

'This is going to be easy,' I thought.

My daughter Katie and I had a map with little red squares marking the location of checkpoints, and the challenge was simply to decide on the quickest route between them. Using a compass to guide us, we had to race against the clock to visit each one and find our way back to the start.

Katie and I set off with great enthusiasm. A short but frustrating while later, I realised that, although my map-reading is pretty good, my ability to walk in a straight line is sadly lacking. I would line up the blue lines on the map with the north-pointing needle on the compass, point confidently in the direction of the next little red square and then head off (child now trailing behind). But then, somehow, we'd veer off, distracted by the presence of a well-worn path or the sight of a family heading purposefully in another direction, and once again we'd find the wrong checkpoint, or no checkpoint at all.

Eventually, I realised that what I needed to do was keep checking that the map we were following lined up with the needle on the compass, and keep checking that we were walking in the right direction.

> *Let us run with perseverance the race marked out for us,*
> *fixing our eyes on Jesus,*
> *the pioneer and perfecter of faith.*
> HEBREWS 12:1–2

Running the race of life isn't just about keeping going; it's also about staying true to the path marked out and continually checking in with Jesus to make sure we haven't wandered off. It's about being sure we're running *our* race, not someone else's; going the way we're called, not the way that looks easiest; and keeping our eyes on the one who went first and has already completed the race.

When it comes to the life-race, even if you do go a little bit off course, there's always a way back. It probably doesn't matter in which order you visit each checkpoint, or even whether you get to any of them at all, only that you keep asking Jesus, 'Which way should I go next?', and that you make it home in the end.

FOR YOUR *JOURNAL* ———————

Which do you find harder, regularly fixing your eyes on Jesus to get a big-picture perspective about where you are and where he's taking you, or remembering to check in with him as you go along to ask for help or wisdom?

What things are most likely to distract you from the direction God is calling you in?

Winnowing

Wheat and corn have to be threshed – a fairly violent process which loosens the grain from the stalks and chaff (husks and little bits of straw) – and then winnowed – separating the grain from the rest. I grew up on grain-growing land, surrounded by fields of golden corn every summer, but I had no idea about winnowing because for a long time there have been machines that do the job very efficiently.

In biblical times, however, and in parts of the developing world still, the job was and is done by throwing the pile of grain, straw and chaff into the air and allowing the wind to blow away the straw and chaff while the heavy grain falls to the ground.

To winnow is to separate.

In the Bible itself, winnowing as a metaphor is often about God coming and getting rid of sin; about purifying the nation; about blowing away all that is bad.

This awkward and difficult task is part of what we're called to as God's people. It strikes me as important, though, that the pitchfork doesn't poke about and separate stuff while it's on the ground. It has a very specific task – that of lifting the whole mess up into the wind.

The wind itself does the work.

Perhaps you are in a place where you're aware that threshing has been done – that sin or shame in your life has been loosened but is still in there in the mix. What's for sure is that it's not your job to sort it all out on the ground, but that you now need to lift up your soul into the wind of God and surrender to his work and to his ability to do it.

I surrender to you,
casting my sin and shame into the air
and calling on you,
the wind,
to carry it away.

FOR YOUR JOURNAL

Ask God whether you still have sin and shame mixed in with who you are, and for the courage to cast it up into the wind of his presence.

Ask God if there are places in the world around you where he would like you to do some winnowing. Bring some situations into his presence in prayer and ask him to come by the Spirit and blow that which is evil away.

Ordinary beauty

It's unfortunate that 'ordinary' has come to be an insult. Our culture finds it hard to honour the everyday and tends to despise (or ignore) the unexceptional. To be significant, it tells us, you must be exceptionally rich, or attractive, or talented.

And yet, in the Bible, it seems that God doesn't only use people who are exceptionally talented, or exceptionally rich, or exceptionally beautiful, or exceptionally strong or exceptionally clever. On the contrary, he mostly uses normal, faithful, obedient, available, *ordinary* people. Moses and Gideon, Esther and Mary, John and Peter: unexceptional people living run-of-the-mill lives until they encountered the living God.

Like this very ordinary spoon, which was surprisingly difficult to paint because of the intricacies of the ever-changing reflections, light shining on those ordinary people lifted them into the extraordinary. Though they must receive honour for their obedience and willingness to serve, the glory of what God did with their lives belongs to him.

I struggle sometimes with the ordinariness of life. Much of what we all do – shopping, cooking, cleaning, working – feels mundane, especially when social media tells us that everyone else is having an adventure!

But the whisper of the teaspoon is, 'Don't despise the ordinary.'

It took me an hour of looking and sketching and painting to realise how complex and beautiful this little spoon actually is, and how its scratches and dents make it unique. I'd dismissed it in a second as ordinary and uninteresting, yet on closer inspection found that the light dancing across its surface was so complex that it was both lovely and too difficult to capture.

I wonder if a better way to respond to the ordinariness of everyday life is simply to choose to look for the light of God as it plays across the surface.

There's beauty hidden in the ordinary,
blessing waiting for me to find it.
I just need to take the time to look.

FOR YOUR *JOURNAL* ——————————

Do you ever struggle with the ordinariness of life?

Ask God to help you look for the play of his light across the ordinary things in your life.

What things can you think of from the last week where you can see God at work?

Dust days

The beautiful Kyrenia mountains are the permanent backdrop to life in my city. If I get lost (which still happens even after six years here), I look for the mountains to get my bearings. When we've been away, the sight of them makes me feel I'm home.

The sky in Cyprus is nearly always blue, so we can see those mountains as clearly as in this picture. Occasionally, we have some haze or cloud so they are harder to make out, or are partly covered, but it's always obvious where they are.

There was a time, though, when an extraordinary cloud of dust descended on the city and we could barely see the buildings down the street, let alone a range of mountains eleven miles away. For almost a week, our mountains were completely hidden.

In life, there are days when the sky is clear, when you can see God's face as clearly as your own reflection in a mirror. In my experience, there are many more days when it's cloudy or misty, and you struggle to be aware of his presence or hear his voice. And then, every once in a while, there are thick-dust days, when it's hard to breathe and even harder to see.

It took a while, but eventually it rained and all that dust was washed away. As our mountains reappeared, I heard God whisper:

'Look at those mountains… Was there one moment, in all of the week that you couldn't see them, or in any of the times when they've been partly hidden from you, when you've doubted that they were there?'

And of course, there wasn't. Mountains don't just cease to exist because I can't see them. I have *faith* in the existence of those mountains! And God said:

'Well then. Trust me that I am here, whether you can see me or not – you just have to turn to where you know I am, keep walking towards me, and wait for it to rain.'

*Now faith is confidence in what we hope for
and assurance about what we do not see.*

HEBREWS 11:1

FOR YOUR *JOURNAL*

What kinds of things in your life kick up the dust and make it hard to see God?

Sometimes you need to turn to where you know God is, because you know he's there, even when the outline of his face is tricky to make out. Declare to your heart that he is where he has always been. If you're walking blindly towards where you know God is just now, my heart is with you. Take courage. One day it will rain, the dust will be washed away and your view will be clear. Until then, he is still with you.

If today you can see God clearly, then take time to pray for those you know who are living in dusty times.

What's down the back of the sofa?

This is just a theory, and as yet not scientifically tested, but I think our sofa might actually suck loose change out of my pockets when I sit down. It's probably a Swedish furniture company conspiracy.

A brief investigation this morning revealed not only a pile of coins, but also an array of pencils, hair bands, guitar picks, earrings, Polly Pockets, Barbie shoes, teaspoons and socks, plus the TV remote (which was what I was actually looking for). It got me thinking about how, in the middle of everyday life, stuff gets lost down the back of the sofa and we don't even miss it.

I read this recently from Romans 4:18–21:

Against all hope, Abraham in hope believed and so became the father of many nations, just as it had been said to him, 'So shall your offspring be.' Without weakening in his faith, he faced the fact that his body was as good as dead – since he was about a hundred years old – and that Sarah's womb was also dead. Yet he did not waver through unbelief regarding the promise of God, but was strengthened in his faith and gave glory to God, being fully persuaded that God had power to do what he had promised.

Abraham held on to that promise that he had heard from God, not letting go of it even in the face of strong evidence that it was impossible. He kept hold of it through years of waiting and held on to it even when it became clear that he had seriously messed up. He held on to that promise and kept giving glory to God for what he was *going to do*.

Abraham didn't let the promise of God go slipping quietly out of his pocket and into the forgotten realms of the back of the sofa.

Today, my friends, is a great day for searching again for the things God has said to you, for the promises he's spoken. It's a day for holding those promises up to the light and blowing the dust from them. It's a day for choosing to give glory to God for what he has promised and for being 'fully persuaded that God has power to do what he promised'. I'm not saying that today is necessarily the day that you step into the fulfilment of all those promises. Faith shows up in the waiting.

But although Abraham, man of faith, waited a long, long time, he did so with the promise of God in his hand.

FOR YOUR *JOURNAL*

What do you think makes you let go of things God has promised you in the past?

Pray and ask God to remind you of any words he has given you that you need to rediscover and hold on to.

How can you hold on to those promises like Abraham did and not let them slip away?

Willow basket

When it's dry, willow is just so many sticks: brittle, stubborn, prickly, awkward, broken in places and very much in need of being bent into shape. I've often felt rather like it.

And yet this is a basket made from willow. It can both hold a harvest and carry a feast. It is strong. It is still what it once was, but also completely transformed.

God and I have talked many times about the process of transformation that makes useless sticks into a beautiful basket. And I always end up with these two 'keys' to becoming: 'soaking' and 'surrender'.

Willow must be soaked, preferably overnight, to make it flexible. Otherwise, when the weaver attempts to bend it or twist and wind it between the uprights, it will simply snap.

Dry willow is brittle and inflexible; soaked willow is soft and pliable.

I need soaking.

I need to immerse myself in God's presence and in his word. I read once that we are like pendulums; we need to swing between abiding in God and working; worship and ministry; backwards and forwards. Not spending enough time in God's presence will make my heart brittle again, but time soaking him in will quickly soften it up.

And as he softens my heart, I become more and more ready to be transformed into the shape he wants for me. But even then, I need to be willing to let him.

In my willow-ness, most of my task is to surrender. Some of my stubbornness has been soaked out, but most of my determination remains. I have to choose to allow the weaver to create whatever shape he has in mind for me and not to insist on becoming something else.

I need to surrender.

Maker,
soak me in your presence
until my heart is soft enough
to yield to your will.
Help me to become
more than I am
without you.

FOR YOUR JOURNAL ───────────────

Do you find it easy to make time to spend in God's presence?

What things do you do to help you 'soak'?

What things do you think God wants to shape in you at the moment? Patience? Confidence? Faith? Gentleness? Resilience?

Colander days

It's all very well standing before God and asking him to fill me up again when I feel like a bucket. Even if I've run completely dry and empty, I can gather together the faith that the Holy Spirit is good at filling me up with his presence, peace and power, and stand there and let it happen.

But sometimes it's harder. Battle, tiredness, stress and disappointment can leave me feeling a bit like this colander – full of holes.

And when that happens, asking God to fill me feels a bit hopeless. I mean, how do you *fill* a colander?

And that's a real shame, because just at the moment that I need him the most, to fill and clean and refresh and *mend* me, I don't have the faith to walk into his presence and ask him to.

So, the last time I had a colander day, I asked God, 'How is this supposed to work? How can you fill me when I'm so beaten up and full of holes?'

His answer was simple: 'Call on me more. I can fill you faster than you can leak.'

Even on colander days.

Actually, I suspect that I'm a bit colander-ish on more days than I realise. And I get the impression that God is not as surprised by my state of leakiness as I am.

If you're feeling full of holes today, ask God to fill you to overflowing. Don't fall for the lie that there isn't really any point because you're a bit broken and full of holes. He is more than able to fill you faster than you can leak.

Father,
though I am full of holes,
pour out your Spirit on my leaky heart again.
Fill me so throroughly,
so completely,
so generously,
that even though I am still full of holes,
I overflow.

FOR YOUR JOURNAL ————————

What kinds of things make you feel colander-ish?

What helps you to connect with God and enter his presence? What plans can you make for colander days to help you to do that?

First rain day

Once a year, we have an unofficial celebration day here on our hot, dusty island when, after a very long, hot summer, the first proper rain falls. All around you can see the dry, dusty patches of land drinking it in: cracks in the earth being filled, dust being washed away, people smiling as the air feels fresher and cooler.

It feels good.

And it reminds me of how great it is to step into the rainy, overflowing, soaking presence of God again, especially if you've been experiencing the heat of a spiritual desert.

It's not always easy to know how to make that happen, but I found a clue in the way God asked me to paint this postcard. The rain I saw in this picture is embroidered in backstitch, a skill I spent rather a lot of time trying to teach to some eager ten-year-olds at camp recently. In fact, I repeated this phrase so often that I can still hear myself saying it, over and over again:

First you have to go ahead of yourself a bit, in as straight a line as you can, and then you have to come back to the place where you saw the last stitch go in. Ahead of yourself and then back, ahead of yourself and then back…

'Ahead of yourself and then back.'

We go ahead of ourselves all the time, striking out in the things we think or hope God is asking of us. But there are times where the thread is loose, the way forward is unclear or we no longer seem to be attached to the line of what has gone before.

These are the moments to stop and to look back. When was the last time I heard God speak? Where was the last time I felt his presence? We need, as followers of Jesus, to keep on going back to him, to sink ourselves into God's presence again, to connect back into our relationship with him before we can determine which way to go forward.

The wonderful thing is that we can walk right in. The way is always open.

Life is backstitch.
We need to learn to keep going back –
going back into the arms of Jesus,
going back to resting in his presence,
going back to *the last thing we heard him say*.

FOR YOUR *JOURNAL* ————————

When was your last 'rain day'? When did you last hear God speak, or feel his closeness or power?

I wonder what the last thing was that you heard Jesus say. Choose to remember it. Sink your heart deep into it. Let it soak into you, fill you up and then give you the direction to stretch out ahead of yourself again.

Building a swing

Building a swing is the easy part. The trick is in finding a good place to build it. You probably want to look for:

Strength. Find a tree with a branch that is strong. You want to be able to trust this swing, to completely relax in it, and that means it needs to be well able to bear your weight.

Space. Make sure there is room to move. There needs to be space to swing out ahead and space to swing back behind you while all the while you actually stay anchored in the present.

Perspective. Tie your swing somewhere very high up. The higher the branch and the longer the ropes, the higher you can swing. And every time you do, you'll be able to see the landscape around you from an entirely different perspective. Truth revealed.

Shelter. Choose a tree that will give you shelter from the sun; there will be days when you need it.

Joy. As well as building your swing, make sure you take time to enjoy it. Give yourself permission to play – have fun.

Strength, space, perspective, shelter, joy. All things to look for in a swing, and in a friendship.

For me, this is a picture of what friendship with God could be like. It isn't always, but it could be, if that's how I choose to build it.

I don't know which thing you need more of in your life today: strength to carry you, space to breathe and move, a new perspective on your circumstances, shelter from the heat or the storm or just the exhilarating joy of freedom to play.

Whichever it is, it is in God's hand, and he would love to share it with you.

You only need to ask.

So trust him absolutely, people;
lay your lives on the line for him.
God is a safe place to be.

PSALM 62:8 (MSG)

FOR YOUR *JOURNAL*

Strength, space, perspective, shelter, joy. Which of these things have you already experienced through your relationship with God, and which would you like him to reveal to you more?

What things stop you from trusting him fully, or from feeling the freedom to play?

How can you choose to lean more into your friendship with God this week?

Empty hands

There are days when you feel like you have nothing left to give. There are days when you notice that your energy for ministry has somehow evaporated. There are days when you kneel before God with nothing but empty hands.

Those are the best days.

Because those are the days when you remember again that true friendship is not based on how much I can do for you or you for me. Love isn't measured in gifting, or energy, or effort, or results. Love just is.

God loves you.

And on the days that you recognise this truth – that before him your hands are empty – he smiles.

Because on those days he knows
that when your heart is hit by the force of his unchanging love for you,
when it is drawn by the irresistible pull of his open arms,
on those days you will understand the miracle of grace.

We have this treasure in [otherwise empty] jars of clay
to show that this all-surpassing power is from God
and not from us.
2 CORINTHIANS 4:7

FOR YOUR JOURNAL ——————

Do you ever feel empty-handed before the Lord?
How do you react when that happens?

How can you encourage yourself and others to rejoice
in his strength and ability to use you in those moments
when you feel weak or useless?

Pomegranates

Have you ever seen a tree so laden with fruit that it's bowing under the weight? Try as it might, this tree will never produce a lemon, or cherries, or a sweet, juicy nectarine, but it's overflowing with pomegranates! Those other fruits are wonderful, and I'm grateful that there are trees that grow them. But these deep red pomegranates, full to bursting with sweet seeds, are beautiful too.

We often waste so much time and energy trying to be or do something other than what God has made us for. There's something really powerful about seeking out what kind of fruitfulness God has for you in the particular season you're in and then not wasting time or energy trying to do or be something else.

The other thing you'll notice, if you find a pomegranate tree in season, is that the fruitfulness you long for can also be hard work when you get it. The branch that carries this fruit has taken time to mature and grow strong enough to bear it, but still, it's bowing a little under the weight.

Sometimes fruitfulness is tiring: doing the things God is calling you to do, investing in the people God has given you, making the choices he is challenging you to make; all those things weigh heavily. But it doesn't mean you're getting it wrong – just that you need to ensure you make time to retreat into God's presence to be filled and strengthened. Just like this tree that needs to have a prop or two under its branches to support the weight of its fruit, so we need to learn to lean back into Jesus and let him shoulder the burden of our harvest.

Creator,
open my eyes to see who you're calling me to be;
soften my heart to the harvest you've given;
strengthen my limbs so that I can bear fruit;
and teach me how to let you take the weight.

FOR YOUR *JOURNAL* ———————————

Have you ever felt your arms bowing under the weight of the challenges and opportunities God has given you?

How can you lean back into Jesus and let him take some of the weight?

When all is not lost

You may recognise this smile from my book *Postcards from Heaven* (BRF, 2016), when one of the front teeth was missing. Three years on, it's full of big teeth, and their somewhat irresponsible owner now wears a (very-expensive-to-replace) removable palate-expander-thingy.

My family were having a fantastic day at the zoo and it wasn't until we were just about to feed a magnificent giraffe that the gorgeous Chaos-Generator turned and grinned at me, revealing a telltale lack of wire.

'Where's your brace,' I yelled, 'and why isn't it in your mouth?'

Fellow parents of wonky-toothed children may recognise the scene that followed. After an intensive hunt through bags and pockets and some frustrated remonstrations, I left the kids with their grandma and unenthusiastically retraced my steps around the zoo, wondering where on earth she could have taken it out and dropped it.

After 30 minutes of hunting, the last tiny bit of hope I had left drained away as I sat down at a table in a woodchip-strewn picnic area, convinced that we would never see the thing again.

And then I looked down, and there it was, just next to my foot.

I'm not sure now whether it had been there all along, or whether God had moved it there. But as I picked it up, flooded with relief, I heard God whisper, 'I am the God who restores.'

'*I am the God who restores.*'

It's funny because I would have said I knew God as Restorer well already, and I do, but in the sense of a restorer of a master painting – someone who comes in and painstakingly cleans something up and carefully repairs damage. But obviously I only had part of the picture.

When I looked it up, the first definition of restore that I found was 'to give back or return'.

Part of what God longs to do as our great Restorer is to return to us things that have been taken away, things that feel forever lost.

Perhaps there are parts of your heart, your confidence, your strength, your faith or your hope that feel as though they have been taken away and are gone. There are times in life when difficult things happen to us and something good that we have is taken away; we make a mistake and some part of us is lost. If that sounds familiar, hear this:

Our God is the God who restores.

FOR YOUR *JOURNAL* ────────

Is there something that you feel has been taken from you that you'd like to have back? Confidence? Faith? Ability to trust? Resilience?

Is there someone you need to forgive for their part in taking something good from you?

Pray and ask God what he would like to restore to you today.

Time to put the kettle on

This huge copper kettle was kept filled and warm on the edge of the range at all times in a Victorian kitchen so that it could be boiled and poured out at a moment's notice. It served the needs of the whole household, providing not only tea but also hot water for cleaning, washing-up and bathing.

We are each like this big copper kettle.

We are designed to serve the family, the body, of Christ each in our own way. Being shined-up and visible on the shelf of the household is much less important than doing the job we were made for. This is not necessarily something I find easy, but it's true.

We are like this kettle.

We need to remember, to keep remembering, that we don't have the capacity to power ourselves. I am entirely dependent on God for the power I need to do the job I was made for. And to receive that energy, I need to be close to him. The only way for this kettle to come to the boil is to *rest* on the hotplate. Every single time it needs to come to the boil, it has no choice but to come back into that place of rest. To be always 'ready', so that it stays warm all the time and can be brought to the boil quickly, it must keep coming back to resting on the hotplate regularly, and never venture very far away from it.

I am like this kettle.

The way I behave, the choices I make, matter. Character matters because it matters what you're made of. Someone chose to make this kettle from copper because it was strong, able to take the weight of the water; because it wouldn't corrode and fall apart or melt on to the stove; and because it is fantastic at conducting heat. I need to be good not only at resting in God and absorbing 'heat' from him, but also at passing that heat on to others. I need to have a character that will not corrode over time or lose strength and melt. It matters what I'm made of.

FOR YOUR *JOURNAL*

Resting in God is important. How are you going to make time to rest in him this week?

It matters what you're made of. Ask God about your character and how he would like to see you grow so that you can be even better at serving him and his people.

When I'm with you

When I'm with you, I'm with an army.

A while ago, this line slipped into my heart and set up camp.

It says, when I'm with you, I can face anything, because I know I'm not facing it alone. When I'm with you, I can be brave and courageous, because I know I have backup.

When I'm with you, I'm with an army.

It's a statement of faith, a statement that slices through fear. And better than that, in Christ it's actually true: one of the names of God that describes who he is and what he is like is 'the Lord of hosts'. It's used more than 200 times in the Old Testament, is sometimes translated 'Almighty', and means that God has ultimate power over all created things, including the mighty angelic host of heaven.

> *The Lord of hosts is with us;*
> *the God of Jacob is our refuge.*
> PSALM 46:11 (NRSV)

What a beautiful, awesome verse. Pause with it for a moment. Read it again. Drink it in.

God is both a refuge – somewhere you can run to and be safe – and the leader of a mighty army who will fight alongside you. He is your shield and the sword in your right hand. He will defend you and he will fight for you. He is *with you* and, when he is with you, there is a whole host of heaven that stands with you too.

Are you fighting a battle?

Sometimes it feels like I'm fighting several skirmishes on several different fronts. It's tiring and painful and I easily forget the mighty army that stands with me and fights alongside me. I often make the mistake of thinking that I'm fighting my battles alone.

Sometimes the reality is harder to see than the deception.

And yet this is the truth: when Jesus is with me, I'm with an army.

FOR YOUR JOURNAL ——————

What difference does it make to you to remember that the Lord of hosts is fighting alongside you in your battle?

Which do you feel like you need most at the moment: his shield protecting you or his sword fighting with you?

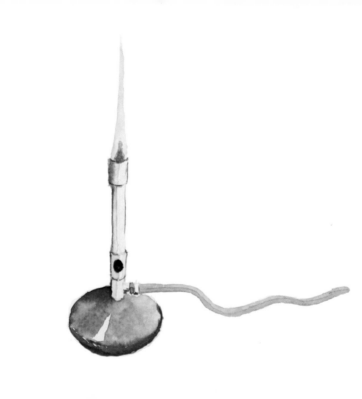

Being open

This picture takes me right back to the first year of high school, sitting at a long bench on the top floor of the science block in a lab coat and goggles and nervously lighting a Bunsen burner for the first time.

In case you've never used one, a Bunsen burner is a very simple and common piece of laboratory equipment used for heating or burning things. It runs on gas and has an open flame which can be controlled by moving a collar at the bottom so that a little hole opens and closes letting in more or less air.

The science is along the lines of the gas needing oxygen to make it burn more efficiently. This hole-fully-open blue flame is much, much hotter than the closed-hole yellow one. If the gas is mixed with pure oxygen, as in an oxyacetylene torch, the blue flame it produces can cut through metal!

This flame is burning much hotter *because the airhole is open to the air.*

It makes me think about my openness to the Holy Spirit and the work he wants to do in me and through me. I so much want to be open so that God can breathe into me and make my flame burn hotter!

What I notice is that it's really easy to let that collar slip around so I become slightly (or very) closed to the Holy Spirit's breath on me.

For me, this picture is a call to be open, to be vulnerable, to the Holy Spirit and his work, so that the flame of our passion and ministry can burn hotter.

Today, I'm going to ask God to show me how open I am to him and the breath of his Spirit, to show me how far the collar is twisted around on the Bunsen burner that is my life, and to show me what I can do to be more open to him. This week, why don't you find some time, *make* some time to be open to God, and ask him to breathe on you again? Bring him your fear, your forgiveness, your pain, your sin and your hope, and in return ask for his life-bringing, oxygen-carrying Holy Spirit. It sounds like a good swap to me.

Burn hotter, my friends, and who knows what you will be able to cut through!

FOR YOUR *JOURNAL* ———————

How hot is your flame burning at the moment?

Which of the killer hole-closers is most likely to stop God breathing through you: busyness, anger at God, disappointment, fear or sin?

Are you aware of needing to repent of any of those things? If so, bring them to him and ask for the Spirit to breathe on you in return.

Changing the ground

This is the plant that would 'never grow'.

Years ago, when my parents moved house, they brought with them a large rhododendron in a wooden pot. The pot was old and failed to survive the move, so my stepfather stripped what was left of the wood away and planted the bush straight into the soil of the garden.

And my mum, who is the only one of us who has any clue at all about gardening, said, 'It will never grow.'

She knew what the rest of us didn't: that some plants need a particular type of soil to flourish. Rhododendrons need to have their roots in acidic soil, not in the chalky clay of an Essex garden. It really didn't stand a chance.

However, 25 years later, here it is – not just surviving but thriving. A great big green and purple horticultural impossibility!

You see, it turns out that even though most of the garden behind my parents' house does indeed have very alkaline soil, the corner where this shrub was planted is in the shadow of a centuries-old oak tree. Year after year, that oak has been releasing hundreds of leaves, which fall in a thick layer over this part of the garden. And year after year, many of those leaves have been absorbed into the soil and have changed it.

The oak tree has changed the soil around it from a place where the rhododendron had no hope of surviving into a place where it has been able to become glorious.

And God said to me, 'Be an oak.'

Because this plant is under the edge of an oak tree, it's alive and blooming, even though the soil is naturally hostile to it. Some people are living their lives, day in, day out, in environments that are hostile to their faith. Conventional wisdom might say that their walk with Jesus has no hope of surviving, let alone thriving.

But you and I can choose to be oaks: continually releasing grace, hope, compassion, truth, faith and love. And even when it feels as though those 'leaves' are just falling to the ground, unnoticed by anyone, they are making a difference – soaking into the soil and changing it.

It lifts my heart to think that I could be an oak tree in someone else's life, quietly releasing what it takes to support life, changing the environment, making a difference. I'm not even entirely sure how, but I'm up for finding out. You?

All is not always as it seems.
Sometimes
you and I
can change it.

*FOR YOUR **JOURNAL*** ———————————

Who has God put near to you who is struggling in difficult soil?

How could you provide shelter and change the ground for them this week?

Butterflies

When I look at butterflies, especially these white ones that danced around me on the breeze as I walked along the canal bank, I find myself drawn into the extraordinary hope of *becoming*. The caterpillar has all the potential to become something beautiful and beyond itself, all wrapped up in an ungainly, flightless body. It goes through a time of slowly feeding and growing, and then an incredibly tough season of transformation, but in all that time it is *becoming*.

One of the most glorious things about being a follower of Jesus is realising that who I am now is not all I'm ever going to be. I can expect an onward journey of becoming more like Jesus, with more hope, love, faith and grace being released into my life. Even when life is challenging and difficult and tiring, I am still *becoming*.

And in that time (and this is the bit I really love), I'm not travelling away from who I really am; I'm actually travelling towards the person I was always meant to be.

In this world obsessed with self-actualisation, I'm letting go of my need to know myself and choosing to try to know Jesus; letting go of my right to be myself and choosing to be who he calls me to be. And beautifully, gloriously, amazingly, this leads me to a place where I become more deeply and truly myself than I could ever have been.

Beautiful.

I'm not who I was yesterday.
I'm not who I will be tomorrow.
But you love me.

Help me, Lord,
to become
fully and completely me,
as you made me to be.

FOR YOUR *JOURNAL* ——————

Look back over the past few months or years. How have you changed and grown? How are you more like Jesus?

What is he growing in you right now through the challenges you're facing?

Do you have any sense of what he's calling you to become now?

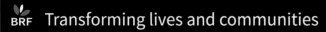

BRF Transforming lives and communities

Christian growth and understanding of the Bible

Resourcing individuals, groups and leaders in churches for their own spiritual journey and for their ministry

Church outreach in the local community

Offering two programmes that churches are embracing to great effect as they seek to engage with their local communities and transform lives

Teaching Christianity in primary schools

Working with children and teachers to explore Christianity creatively and confidently

Children's and family ministry

Working with churches and families to explore Christianity creatively and bring the Bible alive   **parenting** for faith

Visit **brf.org.uk** for more information on BRF's work

brf.org.uk

The Bible Reading Fellowship (BRF) is a Registered Charity (No. 233280)